My mission is to share my true-life experiences to help heal, teach, and restore lives with the words of the Bible.

Dedication

To the parents: thank you for teaching your child of their inheritance in the kingdom of God.

"But Jesus called them to Him and said, 'Let the little children come to Me, and do not forbid them; for of such is the kingdom of God'" (Luke 18:16 NKJV).

To all the little children: Jesus loves YOU!

Mommy talks to a Man in the sky. At night we say our prayers to Him while we are on our knees.

In the morning we thank Him for waking us up. Mommy always says each day He fills our cup.

I don't know when He fills my cup, because I can't see Him. I only see Mommy when she pours orange juice in my cup, or sometimes milk.

then we eat breakfast...

We eat breakfast before I get dressed to go to school. Mommy says the Man in the sky protects and watches over us every day.

I love when Mommy snuggles with me and calls me her little bug. Then she smiles and gives me a big hug.

Mommy told me that this is how it feels when the Man in the sky loves us. I asked Mommy, "Why can't I ever see Him?"

Mommy said, "I'm going to teach you how to see Him. I'm going to tell you the story about the Man in the sky, and how He became our invisible Lord and Savior, so that you can understand why."

I asked Mommy, "What's a Lord Savior?"
She said, "Oh, snuggle bug, that's like being a big mighty king, or a super-duper hero with great power!"

"He helps all kinds of people all over the world. People like you and me, and even the people reading this story!"

"His name is Jesus, and His super-power name is Christ. He's our friend, and He's very, very nice."

"He loves everyone in the whole wide world! Every boy, every girl, every parent, and every grandparent too."

I asked, "What about uncles, aunts, and cousins?"
Mommy said, "Yes, my little bug, anybody you can think of, Jesus already loves them the same as He loves you."

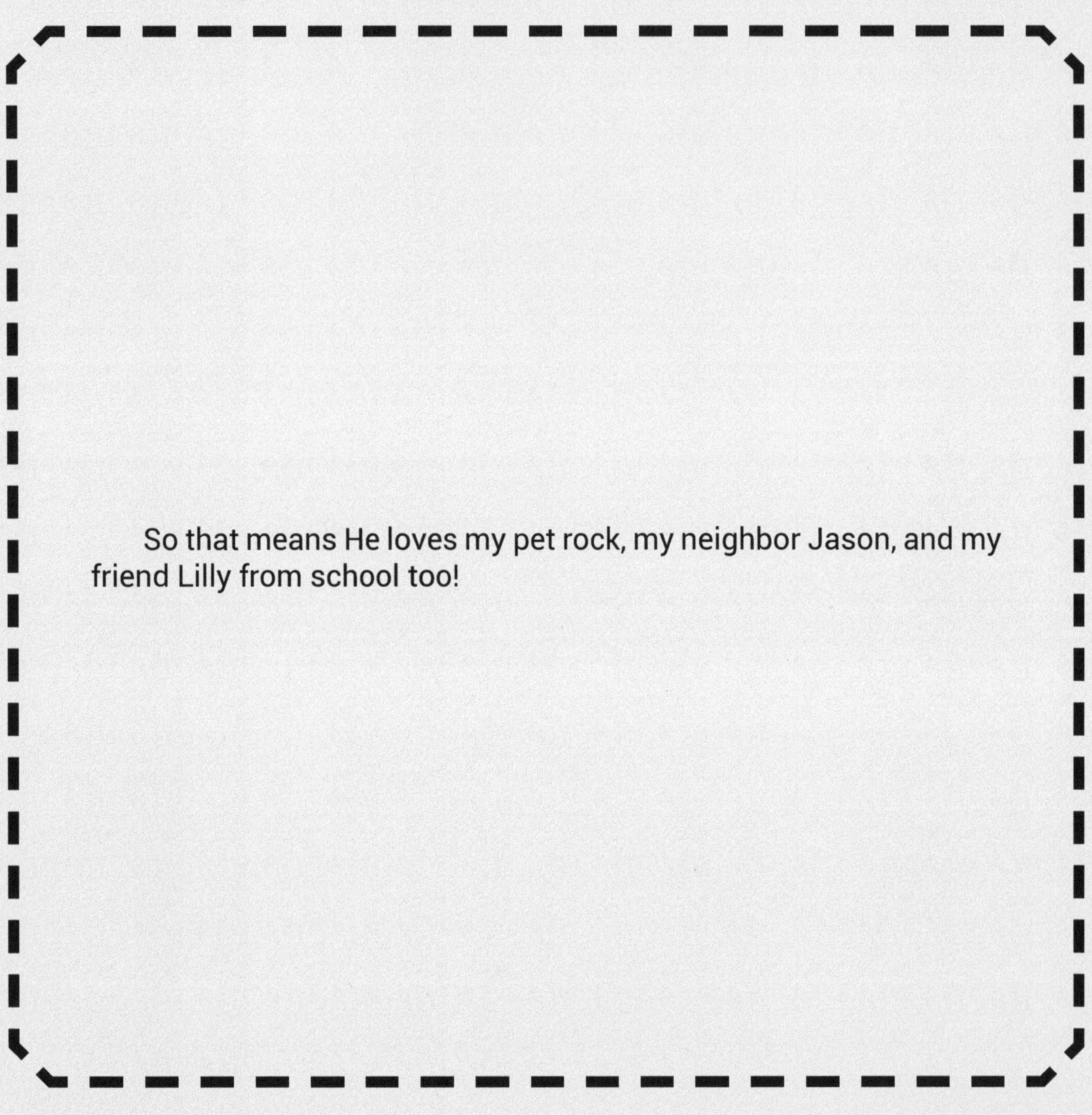

So that means He loves my pet rock, my neighbor Jason, and my friend Lilly from school too!

Mommy said Jesus is so kind, He even loves people who don't like Him, people who pay Him no mind.

Some people don't know about His super powers or who He is, but He still loves them anyway, because His heart is so BIG.

Jesus lives in a kingdom called Heaven, way past the sun, the moon, and the stars. Even past outer space, and past Mars!

"Wow! That's so far away, Mommy. Can we go there to visit Him in a spaceship one day?"

Mommy laughed and said, "No way, not in a spaceship. Anytime that we want to talk to Him, we can just say hello when we pray."

"He will hear us and answer us back in all kinds of ways. When He talks to us from the sky, our hearts can hear Him; then we can reply by saying our prayers."

Mommy reads a special book called the Holy Bible. Jesus talks to us through the Bible by telling us how to pray, how to be good, and how to obey.

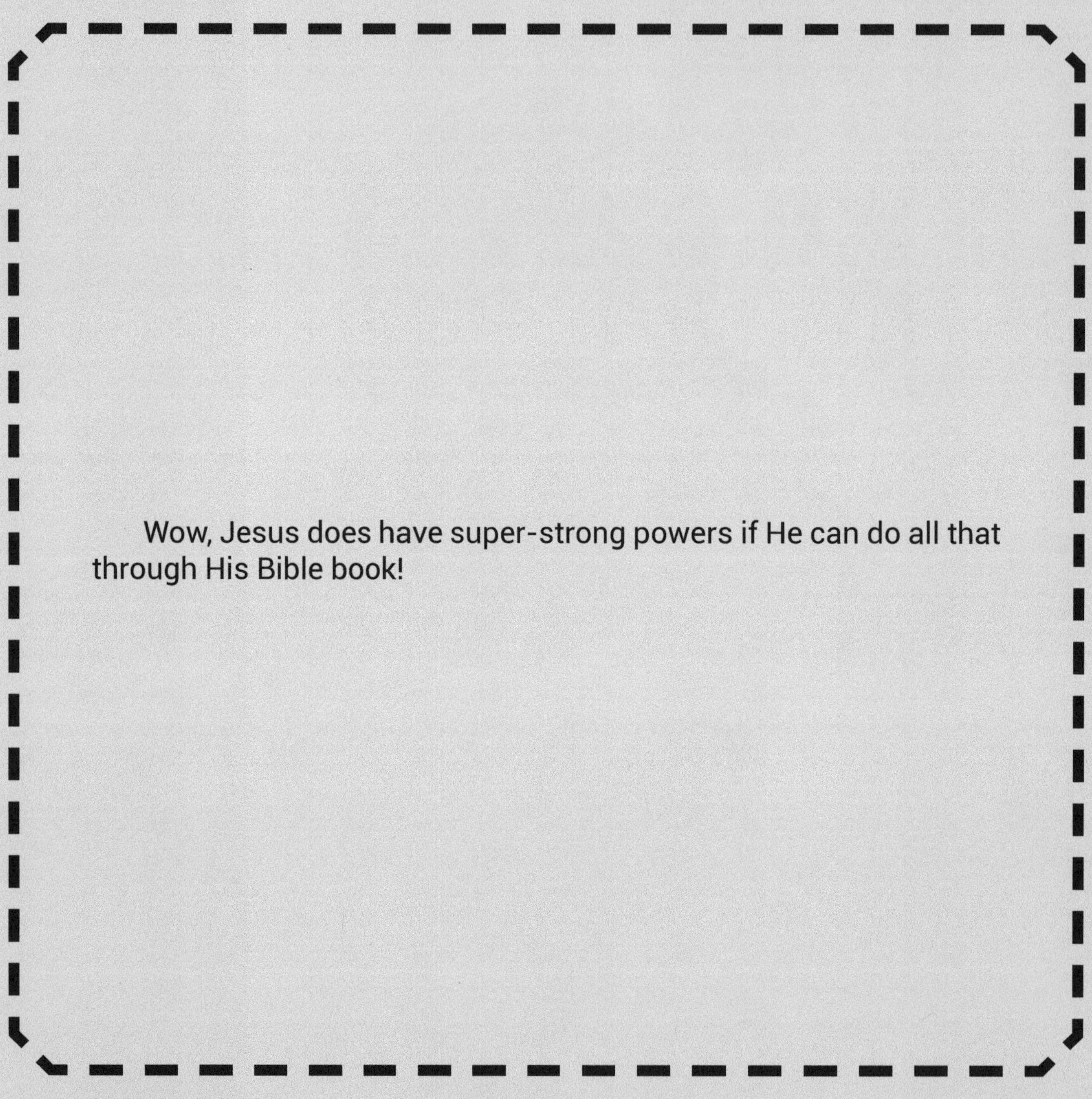

Wow, Jesus does have super-strong powers if He can do all that through His Bible book!

Jesus' Father is God, who loved the world so much. He talked with His Son and told Him that He would send Him to earth.

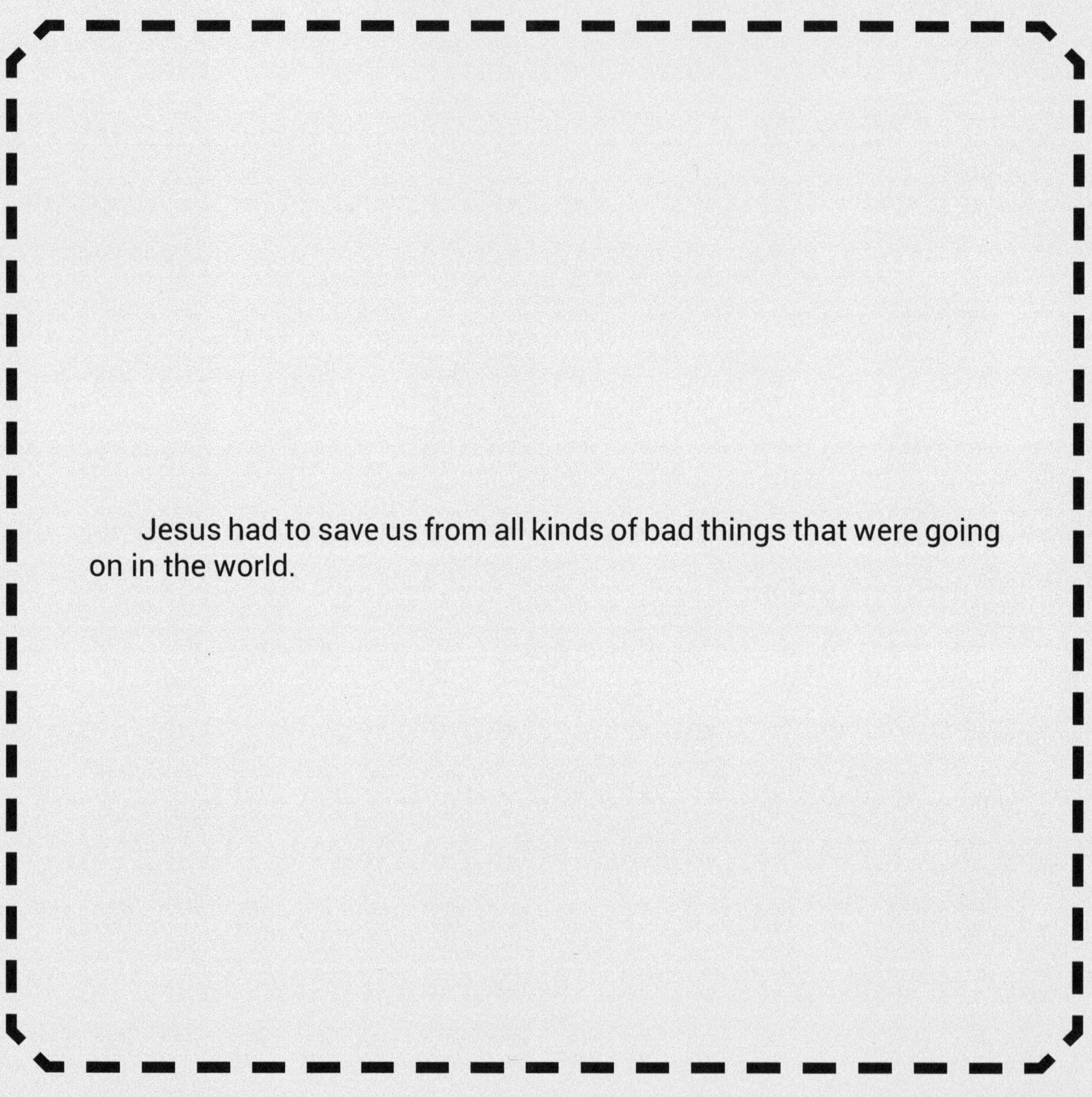

Jesus had to save us from all kinds of bad things that were going on in the world.

Jesus had to remind us of all the good things that we are supposed to do. When Jesus came, He used His power to do all kinds of wonderful things.

    Nobody knew that He was a king. One time He was speaking to a crowd of 5,000 hungry people. He only had two fish and five loaves of bread.

Then He prayed to His Father God and used His power to turn two fish and five loaves of bread into thousands, to feed the people.

26

They even had twelve baskets of leftovers! He fed all the people, and they were happy to celebrate.

Another time, Jesus healed a blind man by making his eyes open to see! Jesus walked on top of the water of the sea; He helped the weak and the poor. Those are just a few things, but Jesus did so much more!

Some of the people did not know who He was, so they told Him to go away; they did not like the things He did or what He'd say.

Jesus told them He was the Son of God. This made Him a king in Heaven. He said, "I have come to help the whole world be forgiven of their sins, so that you can get to know My Father God."

"You can call My Father God anytime, for anything."
I asked, "What are sins, Mommy?"
Mommy said, "Sins are all the bad things we do that God is not happy with, like disobeying our parents or telling lies."

"Because God is holy, that means He can only be around good things. When we do bad things, we have to ask God to forgive us so that we can be forgiven of our sins."

"Some people wanted Him to stop doing all those good things and give up.
One night they put Him in jail. The next day He was hung on the cross with His
hands and feet nailed, and He died on the cross."
"Oh, Mommy, why did they do that mean stuff to Jesus?"

"The people did not listen to Him. But remember, He has super power! Let's finish the story," Mommy said. "They forgot that Jesus was a king with super powers, and that He reigns in Heaven and on earth. He came back alive!"

"He was raised from the dead! Jesus forgave all the people for what they did. He taught them to live the right way."

"Be kind, obey your parents, say your prayers." Then He promised, "One day I will come back to visit! Until that day, I will always be a prayer away." Jesus went back up into the sky, back to Heaven as He said goodbye.

Then the people heard His voice from the sky, saying, "Whenever you need Me, just call My name, for I will never leave or forsake you ever again!"

Remember, whenever you want to help your parents, friends, and family, just pray to God in Jesus' name, and He will help you with His super power!

Whenever you feel scared you can pray to God, and Jesus helps you so He can be right there!
Mommy and I talk to the Man in the sky. Now I know His name is Jesus, but His super-power name is Christ!

The whole time Jesus was on the cross, He was thinking of you! "For God so loved the world that He gave His only begotten Son, that whoever believes in Him should not perish but have everlasting life" (John 3:16 NKJV). You can call His name anytime you want.

Hi Jesus, it's Skylar. Thank you for helping my mom at work...

Let's say this prayer together!

Dear God, thank You for my mommy, my daddy, my family, and my friends. Thank You for always loving us. Thank You for protecting us and being with us forever and ever. In Jesus' name I pray. Amen.

The end.

About the Author

Delicia Mayes received Jesus as her Lord and Savior at the tender age of ten years old at Grace Temple C.O.G.I.C. Delicia started writing short stories in elementary school. In fifth grade, she won a writing contest that awarded her with over two hundred books. She loves writing, reading, art, music, family, and laughter. In 2017, Delicia joined New Beginning Ministries and loves their vision statement: "A Real God for Real People with Real Issues"! Delicia has grown a passion for ministry leadership, and she currently serves on the church administration team and finance team. She sings with the choir, and she also teaches Bible study. She is an active board member of the MCS Fund, supporting sickle-cell individuals. Delicia has spoken at Morning Glory Women's Ministry and several other events with aspirations of becoming a motivational speaker. She has collaborated author pieces in four books with McCurry Ministry International Publishing, two other collaborations with other authors, and has self-published her own first book, *A Back Seat Moment,* where she helped her daughter conquer her trauma from a car accident. She is an experienced MRI and radiology technologist. Delicia has worked in several hospital systems in the radiology department for twenty years. She loves to encourage people during the toughest time in their life. She has a strong prophetic gift; she is not only a voice to the kingdom of God, but a voice to the socioeconomic systems of the world. Her only daughter, Daysha, is an artist who currently attends college at the University of Miami in Florida.

Milton Keynes UK
Ingram Content Group UK Ltd.
UKHW050406010424
440357UK00003B/24